BRITISH RAILWAYS STEAMING THROUGH THE SIXTIES

Volume Eleven

Compiled by
PETER HANDS & COLIN RICHARDS

DEFIANT PUBLICATIONS
190 Yoxall Road
Shirley, Solihull
West Midlands

Printed in the United Kingdom by Netherwood Dalton & Co. Ltd., Huddersfield, England.

CURRENT STEAM PHOTOGRAPH ALBUMS AVAILABLE
FROM DEFIANT PUBLICATIONS

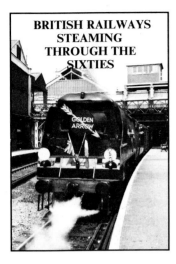

VOLUME 3
A4 size - Hardback. 100 pages
-182 b/w photographs.
£7.95 + 75p postage.
ISBN 0 946857 02 4.

VOLUME 4
A4 size - Hardback. 100 pages
-182 b/w photographs.
£7.95 + 75p postage.
ISBN 0 946857 04 0.

VOLUME 5
A4 size - Hardback. 100 pages
-180 b/w photographs.
£7.95 + 75p postage.
ISBN 0 946857 06 7.

VOLUME 6
A4 size - Hardback. 100 pages
-182 b/w photographs.
£8.45 + 75p postage.
ISBN 0 946857 08 3.

VOLUME 7
A4 size - Hardback. 100 pages
-182 b/w photographs.
£8.45 + 75p postage.
ISBN 0 946857 10 5.

VOLUME 8
A4 size - Hardback. 100 pages
-181 b/w photographs.
£8.95 + 75p postage.
ISBN 0 946857 14 8.

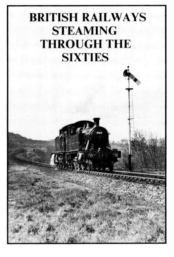

VOLUME 9
A4 size - Hardback. 100 pages.
-182 b/w photographs.
£9.95 + 75p postage.
ISBN 0 946857 18 0.

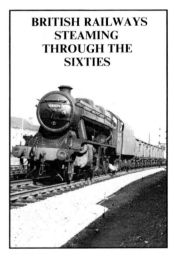

VOLUME 10
A4 size - Hardback. 100 pages.
-182 b/w photographs.
£9.95 + 75p postage.
ISBN 0 946857 20 2.

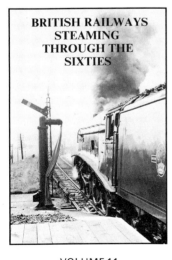

VOLUME 11
A4 size - Hardback. 100 pages
-180 b/w photographs.
£10.95 + 75p postage.
ISBN 0 946857 24 5.

BRITISH RAILWAYS STEAMING THROUGH THE SIXTIES

IN PREPARATION

VOLUME 12

BRITISH RAILWAYS STEAMING ON THE EX-LNER LINES

VOLUME 1
A4 size - Hardback. 100 pages.
-187 b/w photographs.
£9.95 + 75p postage.
ISBN 0 946857 19 9.

BRITISH RAILWAYS STEAMING ON THE EX-LNER LINES

IN PREPARATION

VOLUME 2

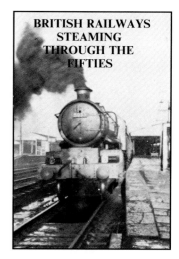

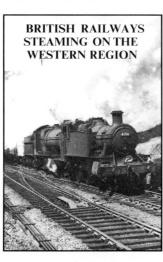

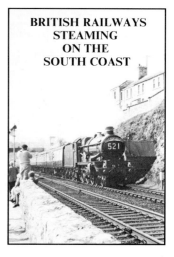

CURRENT STEAM PHOTOGRAPH ALBUMS AVAILABLE
FROM DEFIANT PUBLICATIONS

BRITISH RAILWAYS STEAMING ON THE LONDON MIDLAND REGION

VOLUME 1
A4 size - Hardback. 100 pages
-184 b/w photographs.
£7.95 + 75p postage.
ISBN 0 946857 05 9.

BRITISH RAILWAYS STEAMING ON THE LONDON MIDLAND REGION

VOLUME 2
A4 size - Hardback. 100 pages
-181 b/w photographs.
£8.95 + 75p postage.
ISBN 0 946857 15 6.

BRITISH RAILWAYS STEAMING ON THE LONDON MIDLAND REGION

VOLUME 3
IN
PREPARATION
MARCH 1990

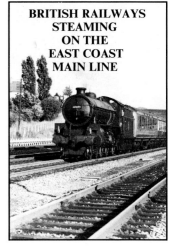

BRITISH RAILWAYS STEAMING ON THE EAST COAST MAIN LINE

A4 size - Hardback. 100 pages.
-183 b/w photographs.
£8.95 + 75p postage.
ISBN 0 946857 07 5.
(Reprinted July 1988)

BRITISH RAILWAYS STEAMING ON THE SOUTHERN REGION

VOLUME 1
A4 size - Hardback. 100 pages
-188 b/w photographs.
£8.45 + 75p postage.
ISBN 0 946857 09 1.

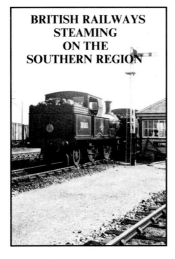

BRITISH RAILWAYS STEAMING ON THE SOUTHERN REGION

VOLUME 2
A4 size - Hardback. 100 pages
-181 b/w photographs.
£9.95 + 75p postage.
ISBN 0 946857 21 0.

BRITISH RAILWAYS STEAMING ON THE SOUTHERN REGION

IN
PREPARATION

VOLUME 3

BRITISH RAILWAYS STEAMING THROUGH PETERBOROUGH

A4 size - Hardback. 100 pages
-163 b/w photographs.
£10.95 + 75p postage.
ISBN 0 946857 26 1.

OTHER TITLES AVAILABLE FROM DEFIANT PUBLICATIONS
PRICES VARY FROM £1 to £3.80 INCLUDING POSTAGE

WHAT HAPPENED TO STEAM

This series of booklets, 50 in all, is designed to inform the reader of the allocations, re-allocations and dates of withdrawal of steam locomotives during their last years of service. From 1957 onwards and finally where the locomotives concerned were stored and subsequently scrapped.

BR STEAM SHED ALLOCATIONS

This series lists all individual steam locomotives based at the different parent depots of B.R. from January 1957 until each depot either closed to steam or closed completely. An attractive book binder is available for this thirteen book series.

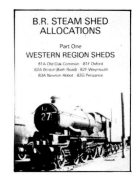

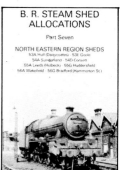

ACKNOWLEDGEMENTS

Grateful thanks are extended to the following contributors of photographs not only for their use in this book but for their kind patience and long term loan of negatives/photographs whilst this book was being compiled.

T. R. AMOS TAMWORTH	B. J. ASHWORTH PENTYRCH	H. H. BLEADS BIRMINGHAM
B. W. L. BROOKSBANK LONDON	N. L. BROWNE ALDERSHOT	J. K. CARTER MILLHOLME
BRIAN COATES AYLESFORD	KEN ELLIS SWINDON	CHRISTOPHER FIFIELD LONDON
A. N. H. GLOVER BIRMINGHAM	J. D. GOMERSALL SHEFFIELD	RAY HARRIS NEW MALDEN
PETER HAY HOVE	R. HENNEFER SUTTON COLDFIELD	
H. L. HOLLAND ST. CATHERINES, ONTARIO, CANADA		F. HORNBY NORTH CHEAM
A. C. INGRAM WISBECH	D. K. JONES MOUNTAIN ASH	R. LEITCH SAWSTON
TERRY NICHOLLS BRISTOL	A. NISBET BRACKLEY	L. PERRIN BOSTON
R. PICTON WOLVERHAMPTON	STUART PITCHFORTH SANDAL	W. POTTER BISHOPS CLEEVE
N. E. PREEDY HUCCLECOTE	B. RANDS WESTON-SUPER-MARE	P. A. ROWLINGS ALCONBURY
M. RUTTER BOWER GRANGE	K. L. SEAL ANDOVERSFORD	G. W. SHARPE BARNSLEY
DEREK SINGLETON ***	C. P. STACEY STONY STRATFORD	M. S. STOKES MARPLE
JOHN STONES TUNBRIDGE WELLS	A. SWAIN WEMBLEY	D. TITHERIDGE FAREHAM
MIKE TURNER BROAD HINTON	TERRY WARD NORTHAMPTON	MIKE WOOD BIRMINGHAM

*** From the Preston Whiteley collection (Kendall) courtesy of David Alexander, Morecambe.

Front Cover — With a clear road ahead, an immaculate LNER A4 Class 4-6-2 No 60009 *Union of South Africa*, from 61B Aberdeen (Ferryhill), makes a spirited departure from Stonehaven with the up *Grampian* express from Aberdeen to Glasgow (Buchanan Street) on 8th June 1965. (K. L. Seal)

ISBN 0 946857 24 5

© P. B. HANDS/C. RICHARDS 1989
FIRST PUBLISHED 1989

INTRODUCTION

BRITISH RAILWAYS STEAMING THROUGH THE SIXTIES — Volume Eleven, is the eleventh in a series of books designed to give the ordinary, everyday steam photographic enthusiast of the 1960's a chance to participate in and give pleasure to others whilst recapturing the twilight days of steam.

In this series, wherever possible, no famous names will be found nor will photographs which have been published before be used. The content and quality of the majority of photographs used will be second to none. The photographs chosen have been carefully selected to give a mixture of action and shed scenes from many parts of British Railways whilst utilising a balanced cross-section of locomotives of GWR, SR, LMS, LNER & BR origins.

As steam declined, especially from 1966 onwards, the choice of locomotive classes and locations also dwindled. Rather than include the nowadays more traditional preserved locomotive photographs in the latter days of steam, the reader will find more locomotives of SR, LMS & BR backgrounds towards the end of the book.

The majority of the photographs used in Volume Eleven have been contributed by readers of Peter Hand's series of booklets entitled "What Happened to Steam" & "BR Steam Shed Allocations" and from readers of the earlier "BR Steaming Through the Sixties" albums. In normal circumstances these may have been hidden from the public eye for ever.

The continuation of the 'BR Steaming' series etc., depends upon you the reader. If you feel you have suitable material of BR steam locomotives between 1948-1968 and wish to contribute them towards the series and other future publications please contact either:

Peter Hands,   Colin Richards
190 Yoxall Road,   28 Kendrick Close,
Shirley, Solihull,   OR   Damson Parkway, Solihull,
West Midlands B90 3RN   West Midlands B92 0QD

CONTENTS

NAMEPLATES — Nameplate examples of the five main representatives of British Railways

1) GWR *Grange* Class 4-6-0 No 6848 *Toddington Grange*. (N. E. Preedy)

2) SR Unrebuilt *West Country* Class 4-6-2 No 34091 *Weymouth*. (A. C. Ingram)

3) LMS *Jubilee* Class 4-6-0 No 45709 *Implacable*. (N. E. Preedy)

4) LNER A2 Class 4-6-2 No 60530 *Sayajirao*. (N. E. Preedy)

5) BR Class 5 4-6-0 No 73082 *Camelot*. (A. C. Ingram)

CHAPTER ONE – 1960

5)   A gleaming GWR *Castle* Class 4-6-0 No 5003 *Lulworth Castle*, from 83A Newton Abbot, stands serenely in Bristol (Temple Meads) station after arriving with an express working from the West Country in the summer of 1960. *Lulworth Castle* was to remain at Newton Abbot until condemned in August 1962. Despite being placed in store during the early part of 1962, 5003 was resurrected in April of the same year but the new lease of life was all too short. (G. W. Sharpe)

7) High summer at Carlisle (Citadel) on 27th August 1960. A less than clean local resident of 12A Carlisle (Kingmoor), LMS *Jubilee* Class 4-6-0 No 45732 *Sanspareil*, helps to add more soot to the already smoke-blackened overall roof, whilst in charge of a northbound express. Judging by the leading coach it was probably a summer extra, added to the normal timetable. (Derek Singleton)

8) The diesels came to 31B March quite early on but despite this mass threat, part of this former Great Eastern shed was to remain open to steam until December 1963. Alive and well, in light steam on 10th April 1960, in the shed yard, was one of the resident ex. GC O1 Class 2-8-0's No 63890, ready for its next duty. 63890 was withdrawn from 31B in March 1963. Scrapping came the following month at Doncaster Works. (N. L. Browne)

9) Bright sunshine highlights the presence of SR Maunsell U Class 2-6-0 No 31621 (70A Nine Elms), travelling tender-first with a guards van at Clapham Junction on 11th June 1960. The class had a total of fifty engines, some of which had been rebuilt from the K Class 2-6-4 Tanks, originally built in 1917. The first withdrawals did not affect the class until 1962. 31621 was taken out of service in June 1964. (N. L. Browne)

10) The name of Heaton Mersey is synonymous with a heavily industrialised area in Manchester and Stockport. As can be seen in this picture there was plenty of countryside within the vicinity of the same. Riddles Class 8F WD 2-8-0 No 90267, from 26C Bolton, blackens the sky with a heavy freight working in September 1960. As can be observed by the overbridge in the background, four tracks were originally planned on this line. (N. E. Preedy)

11) The former Somerset & Dorset Railway shed at Templecombe had changed hands from the Southern Region, coded 71H, to the Western Region in February 1958, being recoded to 82G. Amongst a line-up of locomotives out of steam at the depot on 11th September 1960 were LMS Class 2P 4-4-0 No 40569 and LMS Class 2 2-6-2T No 41248, both natives of the shed. (A. N. H. Glover)

12) The complex but rather run-down depot at 52H Tyne Dock, hosted many steam types, including the elderly ex. North Eastern Railway Q7 Class 0-8-0's, one of which was noted in steam in the yard on 4th September 1960. By August 1961, all fifteen members of the class were allocated to Tyne Dock. This particular class was to fall early victim to dieselisation in the North East, all being condemned in November/December 1962. (F. Hornby)

13)   Tank engine contrasts at 71A Eastleigh on 26th March 1960. Ex. works former London & South Western Railway (Drummond) M7 Class 0-4-4T No 30029, built at Nine Elms in February 1904, dwarfs ex. London, Brighton & South Coast Railway (Stroudley) A1X Class 0-6-0T No 32661, built at Brighton in 1875. Both of these locomotives were based at Eastleigh. (F. Hornby)

14)   The idyllic, tranquil days of years gone by is ideally captured in this picture of GWR 1400 Class 0-4-2T No 1420, from 83D Laira (Plymouth), which has steam to spare at the head of its one coach train at Tiverton on 21st April 1960. 1420 was in charge of the 5.25 pm local to Bampton. This latter station closed in 1963, with Tiverton following on in 1964. Withdrawn in November 1964, 1420 is now preserved on the Dart Valley. (R. Picton)

15) In the late fifties and early sixties, steam was still well in command over the Settle & Carlisle. With steam issuing from the cylinders, 55A Leeds (Holbeck) based LNER A3 Class 4-6-2 No 60077 *The White Knight*, departs from Hellifield, northbound, passing Hellifield North Junction signalbox, with the down *Thames-Clyde Express* on 24th September 1960. 60077 had been equipped with a double chimney in April 1959. (Derek Singleton)

16) A begrimed BR Class 9F 2-10-0 No 92085, from 15A Wellingborough, pays a visit to the massive shed at 18A Toton in May 1960. One of the hazards associated with spotting at sheds, were the point levers, especially at night. Despite the fact that the lever in front of 92085 was painted white, many a spotter used to walk into them, which was quite painful at times. Withdrawn in December 1966, 92085 was cut up at Barry in July 1980. (N. E. Preedy)

17)   A crowded scene at the rear of 82E Bristol Barrow Road in July 1960. In the left background is an unidentified ex. MR
       Class 3F 0-6-0. Nearer to the camera from left to right are: ex. MR Class 3F 0-6-0 No 43444, then a trio of LMS Class
       3 2-6-2 Tanks Nos 40161, 40171 and 40098 and finally GWR 4300 Class 2-6-0 No 6350. All were Barrow Road engines
       with the exception of 6350 – 84F Stourbridge. (G. W. Sharpe)

18)   A fine study of an immaculate GWR *Modified Hall* Class 4-6-0 No 7900 *Saint Peter's Hall*, from 81F Oxford, in front
       of the shed at 82C Swindon on 20th March 1960. Outshopped from the nearby Works, *Saint Peter's Hall*, had been
       serviced and was once again ready for the road. A longstanding occupant of Oxford, 7900 was to remain there until
       condemned in December 1964. It was cut up on site at 2D Banbury in April 1965. (A. N. H. Glover)

19) With steam still in command, SR Unrebuilt *Battle of Britain* Class 4-6-2 No 34086 *219 Squadron* (73A Stewarts Lane), heads the down *Golden Arrow* Pullman train through Ashford, at speed, in March 1960. Transferred to 72A Exmouth Junction in May 1961, *219 Squadron* was to remain unrebuilt, being withdrawn from 70D Eastleigh in June 1966. It was put to the torch at Buttigiegs, Newport in November 1966. (Brian Coates)

20) BR Class 2 2-6-0 No 78005, based at 89C Machynlleth and an unidentified GWR *Manor* Class 4-6-0 get to grips with Talerddig bank whilst in charge of the *Cambrian Coast Express* in August 1960. Talerddig station, situated between Dovey Junction and Moat Lane Junction, on the former Cambrian Railway, closed in 1965. 78005 demised in September of the previous year, being withdrawn from 85B Gloucester (Horton Road). (G. W. Sharpe)

21) A splendid side-shot of LNER A2/3 Class 4-6-2 No 60524 *Herringbone* (50A York) at the south end of York station with an up express in October 1960. *Herringbone* was the last of the Thompson Pacifics, being built in 1947. It was transferred to the Scottish Region in December 1962 being allocated to 61B Aberdeen (Ferryhill) and ended its days of service at 66A Polmadie (Glasgow) in February 1965. (N. E. Preedy)

22) The ultimate in Southern Pacific power at 70A Nine Elms in June 1960. A Nine Elms based SR Rebuilt *Merchant Navy* Class 4-6-2 No 35020 *Bibby Line* awaits its next duty in the shed yard. Constructed in June 1945, *Bibby Line* was rebuilt at Eastleigh Works in April 1956. Remaining at Nine Elms until September 1964, 35020 moved on to 70G Weymouth, from whence it was condemned in February 1965. (G. W. Sharpe)

23)   Warm summer sunshine envelopes this panoramic view of the shed and yard at 88C Barry on 19th June 1960. Peeping out of the shed building are two unidentified GWR 5600 Class 0-6-2 Tanks. Side by side in the foreground are GWR 5700 Class 0-6-0PT No 7766 and GWR 5600 Class 0-6-2T No 5614. Both engines were allocated to Barry. 7766 was withdrawn later in the year and 5614 moved on to pastures new in September 1961. (A. N. H. Glover)

24)   A work-stained LMS Hughes Class 6P5F 'Crab' 2-6-0 No 42931, from 24J Lancaster (Green Ayre), sweeps through Gargrave, between Hellifield and Skipton, with an eight coach summer extra, consisting of mixed stock, on 6th August 1960. The neatly kept platforms and distant signalbox help to complete this picture. 42931 ended its days as a pile of scrap at Cashmores, Great Bridge in December 1964. (Derek Singleton)

25) LMS *Coronation* Class 4-6-2 No 46226 *Duchess of Norfolk*, allocated to 12A Carlisle (Kingmoor), complete with a rather bedraggled train reporting number, speeds light engine, past the camera at Carlisle in June 1961. *Duchess of Norfolk* had been transferred to Kingmoor from its sister shed at 12B Upperby in March of this same year. It remained on Kingmoor's books until made surplus to requirements in October 1964. The end came at the West of Scotland Shipbreaking Co., Troon in February 1965. (G. W. Sharpe)

26)   A haze of white smoke and steam obscures part of the boiler, cab and tender of LNER A4 Class 4-6-2 No 60013 *Dominion of New Zealand* (34A Kings Cross) at Cambridge on 26th March 1961. *Dominion of New Zealand* was in charge of an empty stock (diversion) working on this date. A unique feature of 60013 was that it was fitted with a very deep two tone chime whistle compared with the other members of the class. (R. Leitch)

27)   More Pacific power – this time in the shape of a not very clean BR *Britannia* Class 4-6-2 No 70030 *William Wordsworth*, a visitor to 30A Stratford on 20th April 1961, from 32A Norwich. Next to *William Wordsworth* is an unidentified LNER B1 Class 4-6-0. 70030 moved on to 31B March in June 1961, leaving the Eastern Region for good two years later. It served at three London Midland Region sheds until being condemned in June 1966. (D. K. Jones)

28) An unusual visitor to 86B Newport (Pill) on 16th July 1961, was GWR 4500 Class 2-6-2T No 4557, from far away 87H Neyland in West Wales. It is possible that 4557 found itself at Pill, whilst in transit to Swindon Works as withdrawal from normal service was over twelve months away in September 1962. Stored at Neyland until around July 1963, 4557 was cut up at Hayes, Bridgend in August 1963. (A. N. H. Glover)

29) A derelict building at Derby Works looks down upon an equally derelict LMS Class 2P 4-4-0 No 40682 on 18th June 1961. Withdrawn from 16A Nottingham in February 1961 it had lain in store there until towed to Derby. Stripped of its coal supply, 40682, still carrying its old BR logo, was awaiting the final journey to Looms of Spondon for cutting up in August 1961. (A. N. H. Glover)

30)   A plume of pressurised steam is blasted skywards, disturbing overhead power cables, from the safety valves of LNER A4
       Class 4-6-2 No 60017 *Silver Fox* (34A Kings Cross) as it accelerated the 2.10 pm Leeds to Kings Cross express towards the
       camera in July 1961, near to Sandal on the outskirts of Wakefield. Sandal station had closed in 1957. (Stuart Pitchforth)

31)   New Forest ponies graze unheeding as the Brockenhurst to Lymington branch train rattles past on its way down the
       branch. By 10th June 1961, the converted former London & South Western bogie coaches had been replaced by pre-war
       Maunsell Southern Railway main line stock, adapted for push and pull working, but the engine was still 'South Western'
       – SR M7 Class 0-4-4T No 30052, from Nine Elms. (Peter Hay)

32)   A 16D Annesley based BR Class 9F 2-10-0 No 92072 finds itself on a running in turn on 2nd September 1961. The stubby upper quadrant shows that the road is clear for 92072 as it passed through Oxenholme with a loose-coupled freight. 92072 was destined to remain at Annesley until June 1965 when it was drafted to 16E Kirkby where it ended its days in January 1966. (Derek Singleton)

33)   A gloomy day 'inside' the open shed at 70A Nine Elms on 25th February 1961. Locally based SR Unrebuilt *West Country* Class 4-6-2 No 34020 *Seaton* looks as grimy as its surroundings. Built in December 1945, *Seaton* was never rebuilt and its working days were brought to an end in September 1964, being based at 83D Exmouth Junction, after being transferred there from Nine Elms in May 1962. (N. L. Browne)

34) Not long having emerged from the likes of Crewe, Derby or Horwich Works after overhaul, LMS Class 8F 2-8-0 No 48530, from 18A Toton, found itself in the shed yard at 55E Normanton, where it was photographed on 28th May 1961. Note that the shedplate had not been re-attached to 48530. Between May 1962 and condemnation in March 1966, 48530 was based at four further depots in the Midland Division. (A. N. H. Glover)

35) Smoke swirls from the chimney of an absolutely filthy GWR *Hall* Class 4-6-0 No 4997 *Elton Hall* (84B Oxley), as it prepared to depart from Basingstoke with a Reading train on 12th March 1961. Basingstoke was no stranger to former Great Western power, with locos mostly originating to and from the Oxford area. Bearing in mind the external state of *Elton Hall* it was not surprising that it was withdrawn towards the end of 1961. (F. Hornby)

36) WD Class 8F 'Bed-Iron' 2-8-0 No 90035 (40B Immingham) lays a screen of sulphur over the countryside to the east of Barnetby with up Class J empty flats on 17th April 1961. Judging by the external condition of the engine there could not have been many cleaners based at Immingham at this moment of time. Having said that, 90035 was a particular favourite of the shed and was not transferred away until September 1965. (B. W. L. Brooksbank)

37) The 'Lancing Belle' was a daily staff train from Brighton to Lancing Carriage & Wagon Works. To avoid delaying the intensive electric service on the evening return journey, which was gently but continuously uphill, it was double-headed, in May 1961 by SR E6 Class 0-6-2T No 32417 and SR E4 Class 0-6-2T No 32503. To the right is SR A1X Class 0-6-0T No 32670 on shed pilot duties. All three engines were based at 75A Brighton. (Peter Hay)

38)	A highly presentable GWR 5700 Class 0-6-0PT No 9659, a local engine, was photographed at 81A Old Oak Common on 27th August 1961, on the 'main line ashpit', an unusual occurrence by all accounts. Behind 9659 is an Old Oak GWR *Castle* Class 4-6-0 which can only be identified as No 503? – On this date three *Castles* in the 5030-39 series were based at Old Oak, all with double chimneys – 5032, 5034 and 5036. (A. Swain)

39)	In steam days there was always a standby locomotive in a siding at 51A Darlington, usually a Pacific, in case of failure on the main line. On an unknown day in May 1961 one of Darlington's stud of LNER A3 Class 4-6-2's No 60060 *The Tetrarch*, in pristine condition, was ready for an SOS, complete with an express headcode. Although equipped with a double chimney – March 1959, *The Tetrarch* never carried smoke deflectors. (Stuart Pitchforth)

40) LNER B16/3 Class 4-6-0 No 61464, a Thompson rebuild of the earlier Raven designed engines, leaves its home base at 56D Mirfield, to take up a freight duty in October 1961. In September 1961 a batch of these engines Nos 61449/61/64/ 68 & 76 were drafted to Mirfield to replace Nos 61411-14/16 & 47 from the earlier B16/1 Class which had been withdrawn during 1961. (G. W. Sharpe)

41) A number of onlookers mill round the station platform at Kents Bank, situated between Grange-over-Sands and Ulverston in the Lake District on a fine summer's day on 29th July 1961. The driver of LMS Class 4 'Flying Pig' 2-6-0 No 43008 (12F Workington) was engaged in conversation with two enthusiasts, one of whom appears to be attempting to conceal his identity, prior to departure with a local passenger train. (Derek Singleton)

42) With a cigarette dangling from his lips, the fireman of a grubby GWR Collett 2251 Class 0-6-0 No 2241 takes things easy whilst his locomotive was engaged in light shunting duties at Hereford in June 1961. 2241 was not far from home, being based at the near to hand local shed (86C). For a brief period between July and August 1963, 2241 was allocated to 72A Exmouth Junction, before returning to Hereford. (H. H. Bleads)

43) One of the coaling plant roads at 70A Nine Elms was occupied by SE Rebuilt *Merchant Navy* Class 4-6-2 No 35010 *Blue Star*, a visitor from 71B Bournemouth on 25th February 1961. Behind *Blue Star* is SR U Class 2-6-0 No 31634, based at Nine Elms. Both locomotives had been coaled but *Blue Star* had appeared to have drawn a short straw for the pick of the coal supplies, as most of it appears to be in the form of slack. (N. L. Browne)

CHAPTER THREE – 1962

44)   A pall of smoke curls lazily into the air from the funnel of a 36A Doncaster based LNER B1 Class 4-6-0 No 61145, seen outside its home shed on 27th January 1962. Despite being in fairly smart external condition, cosmetic perhaps, there is a scorch mark on the smokebox door. 61145 had been at Doncaster for many years but eleven months after this picture was taken, a transfer took it away to 40B Immingham. (P. A. Rowlings)

45) The first main line station out of Paddington is at Westbourne Park, just one and a quarter miles away from the terminus. Almost at the start of its journey on 7th July 1962, GWR *King* Class 4-6-0 No 6007 *King William III*, from 84A Wolverhampton (Stafford Road), accelerated through the station with a heavy express bound for Birmingham (Snow Hill) and Wolverhampton (Low Level). (F. Hornby)

46) Plenty of rivets on show on LMS Class 4 2-6-4T No 42102 as it stands in bright sunshine in the yard of its home depot at 1C Watford on 10th June 1962, in company with LMS Class 2 2-6-0 No 46431. 42102 had been transferred to Watford from 75F Tunbridge Wells on the Southern Region in December 1959. It remained at Watford until the shed closed at the end of March 1965, moving on to 1A Willesden. (D. K. Jones)

47) Flanked to the fore and aft by diesel shunters, a locally based BR Class 4 2-6-4T No 80153, the penultimate member of the class, was in steam in the shed yard at 75A Brighton on 7th October 1962, whilst an official visit to the depot by members of the public was taking place. 80153 moved on to pastures new at 70B Feltham in July 1963. A final transfer to 75B Redhill took place in December 1963. (B. W. L. Brooksbank)

48) A bedraggled member of the Peppercorn LNER A1 Class 4-6-2's No 60122 *Curlew*, from 36A Doncaster, pays a visit to 34A Kings Cross on 11th March 1962. Constructed by British Railways in 1948, *Curlew* was one of the first members of the class to be taken out of service, in November 1962, after only fourteen years or so of main line service. (N. L. Browne)

49) The rush hour on the third rail main line out of Waterloo on 6th April 1962 and not a single electric multiple unit in sight. In a flurry of white smoke SR Unrebuilt *Battle of Britain* Class 4-6-2 No 34049 *Anti-Aircraft Command* (72B Salisbury) hurries the 5.45 pm passenger to Basingstoke through Vauxhall station, near to Central London on 6th April 1962. The first of these modern engines were withdrawn in 1963. (B. W. L. Brooksbank)

50) The 'Old Order' on the Somerset & Dorset. The driver of S & D Class 7F 2-8-0 No 53808, from 82F Bath (Green Park), takes advantage of the warm summer sunshine, as his charge climbed steadily up to Masbury Summit with the 7.00 am Cleethorpes to Exmouth express on 4th August 1962. The first six members of this class were withdrawn between July 1959 and February 1962. The last to survive was 53807 in October 1964. (John Stones)

51) Despite playing a major part in the construction of steam locomotives, Eastleigh, in common with the other major regional workshops, also destroyed them. At all times there were lines of forlorn engines awaiting the cutters torch at Eastleigh, especially during the sixties. SR 700 Class 0-6-0 No 30306, late of 71A Eastleigh, its life's work done, awaited the inevitable at Eastleigh on 15th April 1962. (R. Picton)

52) At first glance it looks as though one of the through tracks at Welwyn Garden City had been converted to 'third rail' as BR Class 9F 2-10-0 No 92189 (36A Doncaster) headed a fitted freight past the camera in May 1962. It was a good job that 92189 had a self-cleaning smokebox, or it too would have been as dirty as the rest of the locomotive. 92189 survived in service until December 1965 being withdrawn from 40E Colwick. (N. E. Preedy)

53) LNER A3 Class 4-6-2 No 60061 *Pretty Polly* (34A Kings Cross) enters Peterborough (North) with the empty stock of a down express bound for the north in May 1962. Constructed at Doncaster in 1925, 60061 was named after a racehorse which reputably was the 'ugliest' horse to ever win the 'Derby'. *Pretty Polly* was equipped with a double chimney in October 1958 and German smoke deflectors followed in February 1962. (L. Perrin)

54) As more and more steam engines became redundant, almost every depot had lines of discarded locomotives, many of which were not actually condemned. Noted in the weed strewn yard at the sub-shed of Whitland in June 1962 were 5600 Class 0-6-2T No 6629 (withdrawn in October 1962) and 4500 Class 2-6-2T No 5520 (withdrawn in September 1962). Both engines had been stripped of numberplates, being replaced by chalked numbers. (N. L. Browne)

55) With a 'knotted handkerchief' firmly affixed, the fireman of LMS Caprotti Class 5 4-6-0 No 44748, from 9A Longsight (Manchester) appears to be concerned with the steam issuing from the front end of his mount as it attempted to depart from Rugby (Midland) with a Manchester to Euston express on 18th August 1962. Observing the problem were a group of young trainspotters. (B. J. Ashworth)

56) The interior of Nottingham (Victoria) was grim to say the least, with soot encrusted tall buildings on all sides, not the best of environments. An equally soot-stained BR Class 9F 2-10-0 No 92011 (16D Annesley), with steam to spare, entered the station with a down Class 6 freight on 12th October 1962. Awaiting departure with an up express was English Electric Type 3 'Bo-Bo' No D6753, from 41A Darnall (Sheffield). (B. W. L. Brooksbank)

57) Fresh from overhaul, the paintwork shimmers and gleams as LNER Thompson B1 Class 4-6-0 No 61223 waits to be steamed and returned to its home shed at 40A Lincoln, from Doncaster Works on 27th January 1962. With the by now lack of interest towards steam by the authorities, it would not be too long before 61223 would once again be in a grubby condition. It was transferred to 40B Immingham in September 1963. (P. A. Rowlings)

58) Several hundred miles away from Doncaster, GWR *Hall* Class 4-6-0 No 6957 *Norcliffe Hall* waited to be re-united with its tender, after emerging from the paint-shop at Swindon Works on 16th September 1962. When entering the works, *Norcliffe Hall* was based at 88A Cardiff (Canton) but after overhaul it was drafted to 88L Cardiff East Dock. Like 61223 it would soon be grimy once more. (R. Picton)

59) A gloomy and misty day at 21B Bescot in the West Midlands on 21st January 1962, where the shed yard was packed with steam, pointing to the probability that it was a Sunday. LMS Ivatt Class 2 2-6-0 No 46421, native to Bescot, is surrounded by LMS Class 4F 0-6-0's and LNW Class 7F 0-8-0's, a large number of which were allocated to the shed. 46421 was to remain at various sheds in the area before withdrawal in October 1966. (P. A. Rowlings)

60) The silhouette of GWR 1400 Class 0-4-2T No 1462, from 83C Exeter (St. Davids) is reflected off the calm cold waters at Hemyock on 24th February 1962. 1462 was shunting its gas lit passenger brake out of the station prior to making a return journey to Tiverton Junction. Note the milk container wagons in the left background. Milk trains from the West Country and West Wales were a once common sight to and from London. (Terry Nicholls)

61)   The Riddles 'Austerity' Class 8F 2-8-0's were introduced during the Second World War and were built, not for their looks, but for the dire transport needs of the day. They were taken into BR stock in 1948 and some members survived in service until September 1967. A begrimed 41F Mexborough based example No 90119 was a visitor to 41A Darnall (Sheffield) on 27th January 1962, seen in steam in the shed yard. (P. A. Rowlings)

62)   The frosty atmosphere helps to highlight the smoke and steam emitting from SR M7 Class 0-4-4T No 30125 (72A Exmouth Junction) as it approached Colyton with a two coach local from Seaton Junction on Christmas Eve 1962. There are plenty of sheep grazing in the field but no bright star!!! There was also no bright star on the horizon for 30125 as it was condemned a few days later. Colyton closed in 1966. (A. C. Ingram)

CHAPTER FOUR – 1963

63) A superb study of the traditional shed scene that was once so common – this example being at 72C Yeovil, with Yeovil
     Town station in the right background, on 3rd August 1963. The centrepiece of this photograph is of SR Unrebuilt *Battle
     of Britain* Class 4-6-2 No 34054 *Lord Beaverbrook* (70E Salisbury) which was having its motion oiled by the driver. In
     the distance, behind *Lord Beaverbrook*, is sister engine No 34067 *Tangmere*, again from 70E Salisbury. Yeovil shed, under
36   Western Region control, changed shed-codes to 83E in September 1963 and closed in June 1965. (B. J. Ashworth)

64) LNER A1 Class 4-6-2 No 60130 *Kestrel* (56C Copley Hill) coasts majestically into Kings Cross station on 11th May 1963, a few short weeks before the end of steam workings into this part of London, with an express from Leeds. Built under British Railways ownership in 1948, *Kestrel* was withdrawn from 56B Ardsley in October 1965 and was scrapped by W. George Ltd., Wath the same month. (N. E. Preedy)

65) Modernisation and rail closures in Scotland during the sixties hastened the withdrawal of vast numbers of older classes of engines, so much so that they overwhelmed the resources of the scrap merchants. The result was that many engines were placed in store for lengthy periods of time. Ex. CR Class 3P 4-4-0 No 54501, once of 65B St. Rollox, seen at 65J Stirling in June 1963, had been withdrawn as early as December 1961. (Ray Harris)

66)	A fine close-up of GWR *Castle* Class 4-6-0 No 5076 *Gladiator* by the coal stage at 81A Old Oak Common, in company with an unidentified GWR *Modified Hall* Class 4-6-0 on 9th August 1963. Note the 'home-made' wooden nameplate – the original having been stolen. *Gladiator*, allocated to Old Oak, moved on to 81C Southall in June 1964 and was taken out of revenue earning service three months later. (A. Swain)

67)	In complete contrast to the condition of the 'Austerity' on Page 35 is this picture of WD Class 8F 2-8-0 No 90449, from 41J Langwith Junction on 26th August 1963, ex. works outside 36A Doncaster. 90449 would have been one of the last steam engines to be overhauled at the Doncaster 'Plant' which ceased repairs to the same early in November 1963. A longstanding inmate of Langwith, 90449 demised in January 1966. (N. E. Preedy)

68)	With the closure to steam on the immediate horizon, the shed staff at 34A Kings Cross had lost all interest in the cleanliness of their once proud and well kept fleet of steam engines, including the majestic LNER A4 Class 4-6-2's. The crew of No 60021 *Wild Swan* take it easy as they sweep under Paxton Bridge on the East Coast Main Line with an express on 9th June 1963. (R. J. Leitch)

69)	A trio of small boys who are enjoying the warm summer sunshine 'spot' the progress of SR Unrebuilt *Battle of Britain* Class 4-6-2 No 34073 *249 Squadron* (70A Nine Elms), with safety valves roaring as it heads homewards out of Yeovil Junction with the 3.11 pm express to Waterloo on 17th August 1963. This photograph of *249 Squadron* was taken from a bridge on the Weymouth line. (B. J. Ashworth)

70)   LMS Class 0F 0-4-0ST No 47004 photographed at Williamthorpe Colliery, near Chesterfield, on 27th July 1963, 'on loan' from 18C Hasland. Time was rapidly running out for 47004 and it was condemned from Hasland, by now coded 16H, in January 1964. It was stored at Hasland for six months or so before being removed for scrapping at Wards, Killamarsh in August 1964. (N. E. Preedy)

71)   A trio of WD Class 8F 2-8-0's are lined up in a siding at 2F Woodford Halse on 6th September 1963, a few weeks before the shedcode changed to 1G. One of their number, No 90563 was one of many allocated to Woodford Halse for use on freight trains over the former Great Central main line. 90563 finally ended up at 8L Aintree, in Liverpool and was withdrawn in August 1965. (N. E. Preedy)

72)   A number of locomotives of Southern and British Railways origins were clustered round the coaling shed at 71A Eastleight on 31st August 1963. At the forefront is SR N Class 2-6-0 No 31837, from Exmouth Junction. Apart from carrying the chalked message 'What Happened to Baby Jane' on the bufferbeam, 31837 was also sporting an 83D shedplate. Exmouth Junction did not change codes from 72A to 83D until 9th September 1963. (N. L. Browne)

73)   GWR Churchward 2800 Class 2-8-0 No 2898, from 81D Reading, emerges from Sapperton Tunnel and begins the long descent down through the Golden Valley to Stroud and Gloucester with a lengthy goods train bound for South Wales on 24th October 1963. 2898 changed sheds to 81E Didcot in January 1964 and after withdrawal nine months later it was disposed of by the Steel Supply Co., Jersey Marine, Swansea in February 1965. (N. E. Preedy)

74) A toddler looks down upon GWR *Hall* Class 4-6-0 No 4978 *Westwood Hall*, an 83D Laira (Plymouth) engine, as it heads a freight past the camera at Bedminster, bound for the Bristol avoiding line on 13th September 1963. *Westwood Hall* departed from Laira in April 1964, going to 83B Taunton. Prior to withdrawal in September 1964, 4978 served at 83C Westbury and 86E Severn Tunnel Junction. (Terry Nicholls)

75) BR Class 4 2-6-0 No 76010, 71A Eastleigh, takes a centre road through Eastleigh station with a train of box vans from Southampton Docks on 23rd July 1963. 76010 had been at Eastleigh shed for many years, apart from a brief break at 72C Yeovil between September 1958 and January 1959. Its final allocation was at 70F Bournemouth, which it went to from Eastleigh in October 1965. (N. E. Preedy)

76) LNER K1 Class 2-6-0 No 62014, minus its rear driving wheels, had been converted to a 2-4-0 wheel arrangement and was in company with BR Class 9F 2-10-0 No 92169 in an almost deserted section of the shed yard at 36A Doncaster on 8th September 1963. Despite losing its rear wheels, 62014 was repaired at a later date and lived on until June 1965. Both 62014 and 92169 were residents of Doncaster shed. (K. L. Seal)

77) LMS Class 6P5F 'Crab' 2-6-0 No 42732, a long-time occupier of 24H Lower Darwen, based there since November 1960, stands outside its home shed on 20th May 1963. Note the absence of part of the shed roof (left), a state of affairs which persisted at Lower Darwen for many years and was never remedied. 42732 was withdrawn from Lower Darwen in June 1965 and cut up at Wards, Killamarsh several months later. (H. L. Holland)

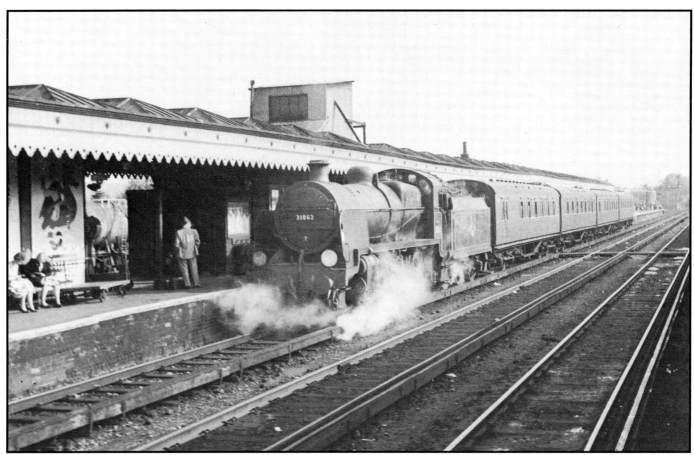

78) Steam was to survive in part at Redhill until June 1965 mainly thanks to the regular work still provided on the services at Guildford and Reading. To the total disinterest of the handful of passengers on the platform, SR N Class 2-6-0 No 31862 was about to depart with a passenger train to Reading in June 1963. 31862, a 75B Redhill engine for many years, was drafted to 70C Guildford in December 1964. (A. C. Ingram)

79) After being ousted from Kings Cross shed in June 1963, the surviving LNER A4 Class 4-6-2's were transferred to 34E New England where the new owners did little or nothing to clean up their appearance. One such example was No 60032 *Gannet*, noted in steam at 50A York on 6th August 1963. In common with Nos 60017/21/25/29, 60032 was withdrawn from New England in October 1963. All were scrapped at Doncaster Works. (H. L. Holland)

80) A lone bespectacled spotter makes his notes in a crowded shed yard at 66A Polmadie (Glasgow) in September 1963. From left to right are: BR Class 4 2-6-4T No 80110, a Polmadie locomotive, an unidentified LMS *Jubilee* Class 4-6-0, LMS *Coronation* Class 4-6-2 No 46240 *City of Coventry* (1A Willesden) and an LMS Class 5 4-6-0 No 45336, from 26A/9D Newton Heath (Manchester). (N. E. Preedy)

81) BR Class 4 4-6-0 No 75054, from 1E Bletchley, powers a loose-coupled freight through the cutting at Ashton, near Roade on the West Coast Main Line on Whit Saturday – 1st June 1963. Despite the ever increasing legions of main line diesels, the line between Rugby and Euston still saw much in the way of steam workings throughout 1963, mostly on freights. 75054 left Bletchley for 5D Stoke in January 1965. (Terry Ward)

82)   The workshop at 81A Old Oak Common hosted the tender-less bulk of GWR *Castle* Class 4-6-0 No 5070 *Sir Daniel Gooch* on 3rd May 1964. This view clearly shows all the fittings within the cab of 5070 including the firebox door which unfortunately was never to be used again to raise steam, as *Sir Daniel Gooch* had been withdrawn from Old Oak in March 1964. Minor repairs were being carried out to enable the engine to make its last sad sojourn to the scrapyard at Birds, Risca in South Wales. (J. K. Carter)

83) The busy station at Preston was all but empty of traffic on April 7th 1964, with the exception of a shining WD Class 8F 2-8-0 No 90699 which had opened up for the climb to the north with a down mineral train from the Wigan coalfields. Recently outshopped, 90699 had been re-allocated to 55E Normanton from 55D Royston after overhaul. It survived in service at Normanton until September 1967. (H. L. Holland)

84) At the other end of the country, nine days earlier, on 29th March 1964, the weather was overcast and gloomy and the subject matter was cold and dead. Surplus to requirements, SR H Class 0-4-4T No 31263, built at Ashford Works in 1905, and SR Q Class 0-6-0 No 30544 had been condemned in January 1964 and were waiting to go for scrap in the yard of their former home at 75E Three Bridges. (F. Hornby)

85) Another view of a condemned locomotive – GWR 2251 Class 0-6-0 No 2221 in an isolated section of the yard at its home shed, the former Great Western depot at Banbury on 15th November 1964. 2221 had been withdrawn this same month and although it had lost its cab numberplates, the front plate and shed-code were still in place. 2221 was cut up at the shed by Friswells Ltd., in March 1965. (Terry Ward)

86) The freight orientated shed at Coalville never hosted any of the more glamorous engine types, nevertheless it was an important part of the railway scene. Its own allocation consisted mainly of the ex. MR Class 2F and 4F 0-6-0's and LMS Class 8F 2-8-0's. A visitor to the depot on 26th February 1964, was LMS Class 8F 2-8-0 No 48133, from 2E Saltley. The shed closed to steam in October 1965 and survives as a diesel depot. (N. E. Preedy)

87)   In the twilight of its long life, LNER A3 Class 4-6-2 No 60091 *Captain Cuttle* (52A Gateshead) was about to clatter over pointwork after passing Retford South signalbox, light engine, heading northwards on 21st May 1964. Note the missing dome cover! Constructed at Doncaster in 1928, *Captain Cuttle* had been modified with a double chimney in October 1959 and the deflectors were fitted in October 1961. Withdrawal came in October 1964. (K. L. Seal)

88)   A less than clean LMS Class 5 4-6-0 No 45109, from 8K Bank Hall (Liverpool), drifts past Blackburn East signalbox and into the station on 28th August 1964, with the 10.32 am Colne to Blackpool express. 45109 moved on to 8B Warrington from Bank Hall in November 1964, remaining there until no longer required, in April 1967. A last journey took 45109 to Cohens, Kettering, for dismantling, in September 1967. (H. L. Holland)

89) Exeter was still a bastion for Southern main line steam during 1964, at least until September when 72A Exmouth Junction lost its allocation of Pacifics. In February 1964, SR Unrebuilt *Battle of Britain* Class 4-6-2 No 34079 *141 Squadron* (72A), prepared to depart from Exeter (Central) with a passenger working. *141 Squadron* was transferred from Exmouth Junction to 70D Eastleigh seven months later. (G. W. Sharpe)

90) An extemely rare 'cop' for Southern fans in May 1964. In steam in the yard at 70A Nine Elms was BR Class 4 2-6-0 No 76079, from 8G Sutton Oak in the North-West section of the London Midland Region. How on earth it had found its way this far south is anybody's guess – perhaps it had been running in after repair at Eastleigh Works. 76079 remained at Sutton Oak until the shed closed in June 1967, whereupon it went to 8F Springs Branch Wigan. (A. C. Ingram)

91) Although rapidly diminishing in numbers, the odd LMS *Jubilee* Class 4-6-0 still survived visits to workshops. Undergoing a major overhaul on 5th April 1964 at Crewe Works, was No 45626 *Seychelles*, from 55A Leeds (Holbeck). During the remainder of 1964, *Seychelles* was a common sight on the former Midland main line from Leeds-Sheffield-Birmingham-Gloucester and Bristol. It survived until November 1965. (R. Hennefer)

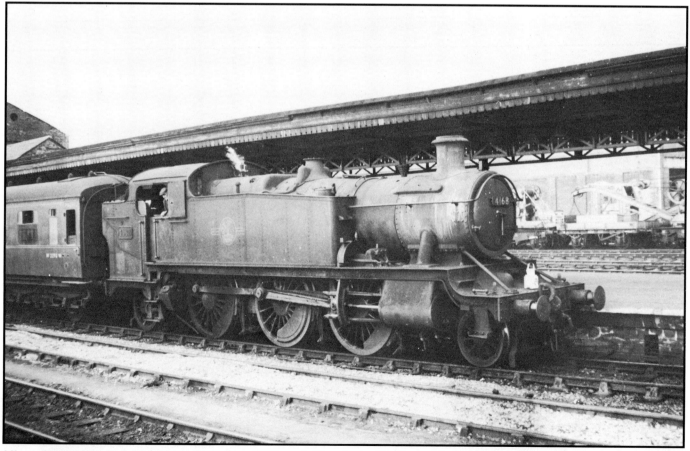

92) GWR 5100 Class 2-6-2T No 4168, from 2C Stourbridge, looked in dire need of a clean-up, as it stood at Worcester (Shrub Hill) with a stock working in July 1964. In the background is a consortium of breakdown cranes. 4168 left Stourbridge in July 1965, a year before the shed closed and was drafted to 2A Tyseley, in Birmingham. Withdrawn two months later, 4168 was eventually cut up at Cashmores, Great Bridge in February 1966. (D. K. Jones)

93) A trio of magnificent Southern Region Pacifics, in the shed yard at 70A Nine Elms in April 1964. Two can be identified as Rebuilt *Battle of Britain* Class 4-6-2 No 34077 *603 Squadron* (built July1948 – rebuilt July 1960) and rebuilt *Merchant Navy* Class 4-6-2 No 35028 *Clan Line* (built December 1948 – rebuilt October 1959). Both engines were allocated to Nine Elms. (A. C. Ingram)

94) A rather bedraggled LMS *Coronation* Class 4-6-2 in full cry on 28th August 1964. The exhaust from the tender denotes that the fireman of No 46248 *City of Leeds* (5A Crewe - North) was using the coal-pusher to bring coal forward as the loco heads south from Leyland, in a rainstorm, with the last scheduled steam hauled *Lakes Express* bound for Euston. *City of Leeds*, in maroon livery, was withdrawn a few weeks later. (H. L. Holland)

95)   BR *Clan* Class 4-6-2 No 72007 *Clan Mackintosh*, from 12A Carlisle (Kingmoor), sweeps down from Shap summit with a fitted freight on 28th November 1964. An early snowfall has dusted the hills and the low sun casts the shadow of Greenholme road bridge (and the photographer – left) across the cutting. Although of modern design, introduced in 1952, the *Clan's* were not considered a success and were all gone by May 1966. (H. L. Holland)

96)   A nostalgic memory of the inside of 50A York's roundhouse on 19th May 1964. The main focus of the camera was of one of the few ex. NER J27 Class 0-6-0's still active outside the Tyneside area, No 65844. Also present and in steam were LMS Class 4 'Flying Pig' 2-6-0 No 43071 and LNER V2 Class 2-6-2 No 60886. All three locomotives were York based engines. On the turntable was an unidentified WD Class 2-8-0. (H. L. Holland)

97)   BR *Britannia* Class 4-6-2 No 70014 *Iron Duke*, in steam in the yard of its home base at 1A Willesden, on 23rd October 1964. With the LMS *Coronation* 4-6-2's now all gone from British Railways tracks, the *Britannia's* on the London Midland Region, filled in the gaps, subject to the non-availability of main line diesels. This they did with admirable results, until they too, were cast on the scrap heap. (N. E. Preedy)

98)   Many of the rural branch lines in England and Wales on the Western Region were still in the hands of steam during 1964, a feature which was to change rapidly once the year ended, with wholesale line closures and new diesel multiple units arriving on the scene. GWR 4300 Class 2-6-0 No 7320 (87A Neath) departs from Quakers Yard (High Level) with a Pontypool Road to Neath local passenger train on 5th June 1964. Closure came this same year. (W. Potter)

99) The warm, hazy sunshine of a summer's day is reflected off the boiler of SR Rebuilt *West Country* Class 4-6-2 No 34040 *Crewkerne*, from 70F Bournemouth, as it approached the camera near to Brockenhurst, in the New Forest, at the head of an express working in August 1964. In the late fifties there were a numerical batch of these engines based at Bournemouth, Nos 34040-46. (G. W. Sharpe)

100) Special traffic brought LNER V2 Class 2-6-2 No 60919, from 61B Aberdeen (Ferryhill), to Perth on 28th March 1964, where is was photographed after servicing in the shed yard at 63A. Despite losing its steam worked services to Inverness in 1962, Perth remained a busy depot, often hosting Pacifics from the BR, LMS and LNER classes. LNER A2 Class 4-6-2's Nos 60527 and 60528 were based at 63A for a short period in 1960. (B. Rands)

CHAPTER SIX – 1965

101) Photographed from the leading carriage of a diesel multiple unit, 62A Thornton Junction based WD Class 8F 2-8-0 No 90350, with safety valves lifting, cautiously negotiates the metal lattice-work of the Tay Bridge with a load of empty coal wagons bound for the Fife collieries on 25th June 1965. Allocated to Thornton Junction for many a year, 90350 was withdrawn from there in August 1966 and disposed of by McWilliams, Shettleston in November of the same year.

(A. Nisbet)

102) A lengthy line-up of various classes in the yard at York in April 1965. The line-up includes a number of unknown LNER A1 Class 4-6-2's, mostly stored or withdrawn. Heading the cast is LMS Class 4 'Flying Pig' 2-6-0 No 43138, with the smokebox door 'bulled' up. Also present is LNER V2 Class 2-6-2 No 60929. Both locomotives were native to York shed. (G. W. Sharpe)

103) It was a sure sign that steam was on the way out when name and numberplates disappeared from locomotives. GWR *Manor* Class 4-6-0 No 7816 *Frilsham Manor*, from 85B Gloucester (Horton Road), in a disgraceful external state, was minus all plates with the exception of the cabside ones as it took the former Midland line through Cheltenham station with a northbound freight train on 26th July 1965. (K. L. Seal)

104) One of the most famous, non-passenger trains, were the Redbank to Scotswood newspaper trains, which in the main were entrusted to steam haulage, often double-headed, until the end of steam. LNER B1 Class 4-6-0 No 61319 (50A York) and LMS Class 5 4-6-0 No 44715 (5B Crewe – South) combine with one of the lengthy empty newspaper van trains at Sowerby Bridge on 6th August 1965. (N. E. Preedy)

105) A miserable, grey day at Basingstoke on 17th July 1965. A group of spotters make their notes as SR Rebuilt *Battle of Britain* Class 4-6-2 No 34090 *Sir Eustace Missenden, Southern Railway* (70D Eastleigh), passed between the shed and a lofty upper quadrant signal gantry, with an up express consisting of London Midland Region stock. Constructed in December 1948, *Sir Eustace Missenden* was rebuilt at Eastleigh in August 1960. (F. Hornby)

106) It took until the end of 1965 for the newer LMS Class 8F 2-8-0s finally to displace the LMS Class 4F 0-6-0's from Newton Heath shed. The last two examples, Nos 44247 and 44544 were dumped out of use, alongside the site of a former turntable on 10th June 1965. 44544 had been condemned two months earlier but 44247 was not officially condemned until December 1965. (H. L. Holland)

107) 9B Stockport was a popular shed for 'spotters', for even if you were slung out by the foreman or shedmaster, which was rare, most of the engines in the yard could be noted from the high bank which ran alongside the depot. Begrimed BR Caprotti Class 5 4-6-0 No 73135, from 9H Patricroft, was a visitor to Stockport on 18th June 1965. The weed overgrown track was a sign of the times – disinterest. (M. S. Stokes)

108) Compared with its more illustrious counterparts in London, the former Great Central Railway terminus at Marylebone was somewhat kept in the shade. A row of dingy tenement buildings look down upon an equally dingy LMS Class 5 4-6-0 No 44666 as it departed from the almost deserted station with the 16.38 to Nottingham (Victoria) in June 1965. 44666 was somewhat off the beaten track, shedded at 2E Saltley. (M. S. Stokes)

109) A batch of LNER A2 Class 4-6-2's were allocated to 66A Polmadie (Glasgow) in October 1963 – Nos 60512/22/24/27/ 30 & 35 and some were still left there after the demise of the LMS *Coronation* Class 4-6-2's in October1964. No doubt they took over some of the duties of the latter whilst at Polmadie. By June 1965, they too had been made redundant and the survivors, amongst them No 60512 *Steady Aim*, were placed into store. (A. C. Ingram)

110) The decline of former Great Western steam is all too obvious in this photograph of GWR *Modified Hall* Class 4-6-0 No 7912 *Little Linford Hall*, in atrocious condition, minus all identifying plates on 3rd July 1965. *Little Linford Hall* was passing Standish Junction with a summer Saturday holiday express from the South coast to Wolverhampton. Judging by the state of the smoke, the contents of the tender were rather sub-standard. (W. Potter)

111) With the forthcoming end of steam on the Western Region in the immediate future, many engines were despatched northwards, under their own power, in multiples of three and four, from Gloucester. On 14th November 1965, a quartet of light engines departed from 85B Horton Road shed, heading for Birmingham. They consisted of two LMS Class 8F 2-8-0's, one which was No 48754 and two BR Class 9F 2-10-0's, one being No 92215. (W. Potter)

112) Although there were still over two years to go before the end of steam at 70A Nine Elms, the atmosphere had an air of dereliction in the summer of 1965. Looking out of the main shed structure and into the vast yard, there were only two engines on view, both local inhabitants of Nine Elms – BR Class 3 2-6-2T No 82029 and SR Rebuilt *West Country* Class 4-6-2 No 34024 *Tamar Valley*. Both survived until the end in July 1967. (D. K. Jones)

113) BR Class 9F 2-10-0 No 92002 (2A Tyseley) was in quite commendable condition, apart from the bent handrail on the smoke deflector, whilst visiting 81C Southall in November 1965, shortly before the shed closed to steam. 92002 was transferred briefly to 2E Saltley after the closure of Tyseley shed to steam in November 1966 and ended its short working life based at 8H Birkenhead in November 1967, when the latter closed. (G. W. Sharpe)

114)   The flat countryside to the north of York provided the railways with an ideal racing ground for men and machines, including those employed on express freight duties. With a wisp of steam trailing from the safety valves, LNER K1 Class 2-6-0 No 62043, from 51A Darlington, coasted along on a freight duty, near to Beningbrough, between York and Thirsk in the late winter of 1965. (G. W. Sharpe)

115)   Aintree, on the outskirts of Liverpool, along with the railways, would have been just another anonymous town, little known outside the immediate vicinity, if it were not for just one small aspect – 'The Grand National' – the most famous horse race in the world. On the day of the race, people from all types of backgrounds converged on Aintree, many of whom were conveyed by train. LMS Class 2 2-6-0 No 46496 shunts the stock of a special on 27th March 1965. (H. L. Holland)

116) It is difficult to assess if the boiler of ex. Great Central Railway 04/8 Class 2-8-0 No 63788 is reflecting the grime and dirt on the ground, or vice-versa, such was the external state of this engine, seen at 36A Doncaster at the end of December 1965. 63788, a Doncaster engine, was in store, prior to condemnation the following month. It was soon cut up, in February 1966, by Wards, Beighton, Sheffield. (M. S. Stokes)

117) Within a few short months, the two young spotters on the platform at Newport (High Street) would no longer have any live steam engine numbers to put in their notebooks. Nearing the end of its working life, 5600 Class 0-6-2T No 6614, from 88B Cardiff (Radyr), trundles through the station with an up mineral train on 6th April 1965. 6614 was withdrawn from Radyr in June 1965 and scrapped four months later at Briton Ferry. (B. W. L. Brooksbank)

118) The driver and fireman of SR Rebuilt *Merchant Navy* Class 4-6-2 No 35003 *Royal Mail*, pose for the camera as their charge drifted slowly through Bournemouth (Central) in an up direction on a centre road, light engine in the summer of 1965. *Royal Mail*, a locally based locomotive, moved on to 70G Weymouth in October 1966. Built in September 1941 it was rebuilt eighteen years later, in September 1959. (G. W. Sharpe)

119) A trio of LMS Class 8F 2-8-0's are lined up in the yard of 16F Burton in August 1965. Only one can be identified, nearest to the camera is No 48368 which was paired with a smaller capacity Fowler tender as opposed to the normal, larger, Stanier type. 48368 had been based at Burton since May 1964. It was transferred to 5D Stoke in September 1966. A final transfer took it to 9D Newton Heath in August 1967. (Ken Ellis)

120) The authorities on the Southern Region must have been somewhat relieved when steam finished in July 1967, for in the lead-up to this sad date the region was invaded by spotters and photographers alike in a frantic effort to log and capture on camera, the last steam survivors. One of the favourite locations was 70D Eastleigh where SR Rebuilt *Battle of Britain* Class 4-6-2 No 34089 *602 Squadron* (70E Salisbury) was noted on 16th August 1966. (D. Titheridge)

121)   The wooded hillsides around Shap echoed to the steady beat of the exhaust reverberating from the chimney of BR *Britannia* Class 4-6-2 No 70023 *Venus*, from 5B Crewe (South) on a rain-soaked day in July 1966. *Venus*, complete with a home-made numberplate and minus name and shedplate, was in charge of a summer extra passenger train. In common with all of the surviving Britannia's, *Venus* ended up at 12A Carlisle (Kingmoor). (G. W. Sharpe)

122)   Part of the inner sanctum at 61B Aberdeen (Ferryhill) contained the repair shop, a once busy section of the shed. We catch a glimpse of withdrawn LNER A4 Class 4-6-2 No 60009 *Union of South Africa*, minus tender, in September 1966, undergoing minor repairs prior to removal to 62A Thornton Junction for storage and eventual active preservation at Markinch in the safe hands of the new owner, John Cameron. (Stuart Pitchforth)

123) The summer of 1966 was to be the last in which steam was to dominate the services from Waterloo to Bournemouth and Weymouth. With the third rails already in position, the fireman, complete with knotted handkerchief, of SR Unrebuilt *West Country* Class 4-6-2 No 34015 *Exmouth* (70E Salisbury), looks back at the curve they have swept through after leaving Pokesdown with an up express on 19th August 1966. (T. R. Amos)

124) The mainstay of the Lancashire local services in the early and mid-sixties were the LMS Class 4 2-6-4 Tanks until their numbers were depleted by the ever increasing D.M.U's. Working wrong line on a frost-bitten 3rd December 1966 was No 42644 (9E Trafford Park) seen approaching Clifton Junction with a five coach 'express' bound for the East Lancashire line. 42644 was withdrawn from Trafford Park in March 1967. (H. L. Holland)

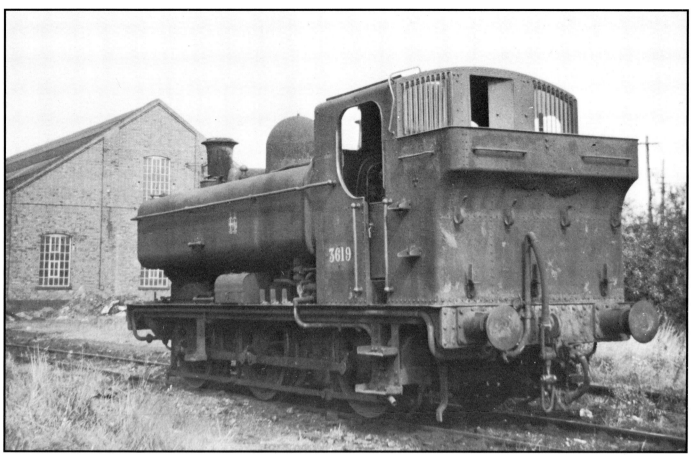

125) By 30th September 1966 the once busy steam shed at Tyseley had been reduced to a handful of active locomotives. It was the end of the road for GWR 5700 Class 0-6-0PT No 3619, stripped of all plates and dumped unwanted on a rusty siding. This former Great Western depot, coded 84E, had been taken over by the LMR authorities and re-coded 2A in September 1963. Tyseley closed to steam on 7th November 1966. (Mike Wood)

126) The Great Western influence at the joint GWR/LNW shed at Birkenhead had long ceased with the departure of 4300 Class 2-6-0 No 6346 and 5700 Class 0-6-0 Pannier Tanks Nos 3626, 3742, 7714 and 9651 to pastures new in December 1958. In 1966 the shed was still very active with a large allocation of LMS and BR types. In light steam in the yard on 29th May 1966 was a Birkenhead owned BR Crosti Class 9F 2-10-0 No 92021. (C. P. Stacey)

127) SR Unrebuilt *West Country* Class 4-6-2 No 34006 *Bude* (70E Salisbury), prepares to negotiate a maze of tracks at Waterloo after bringing in an express from Salisbury in September 1966. *Bude* is reversing light engine to 70A Nine Elms for servicing in readiness for a return journey later in the day. Constructed in August 1945, *Bude* was taken out of service at Salisbury in March 1967. (Brian Coates)

128) A fitter is applying some front end attention to LMS Class 5 4-6-0 No 45488, in light steam at 67A Corkerhill (Glasgow) on 15th July 1966. Also present in this picture are two unidentified BR locomotives from the Class 5 4-6-0's and the Class 4 2-6-0's and BR Class 4 2-6-4T No 80025. Both 80025 and 45488 were based at Corkerhill and were withdrawn in August and November 1966 respectively. Corkerhill shed closed to steam on 1st May 1967. (C. P. Stacey)

129) Sunlight and shadow at 5B Crewe (South) on 27th February 1966. With the closure of 5A Crewe (North) and Gresty Lane depots, Crewe (South) was the sole remaining steam shed at this cornerstone of the LMR. Photographed in the yard on this day was BR Class 5 4-6-0 No 73096, a visitor from 9H Patricroft, in Manchester, with a chalked shedcode. Withdrawn in November 1967 and stored at Barry, 73096 is now earmarked for preservation. (Mike Wood)

130) With steam leaking from many places, a work-stained and smokebox scorched ex. NER J27 Class 0-6-0 No 65835 (52G Sunderland) struggles past the camera with a rake of coal empties at West Hartlepool on 30th April 1966. Condemned at Sunderland in January 1967, 65835 was cut up at Choppinton (Guide Post) by Messrs. Willoughby's in March 1967 after a brief period of storage. (N. E. Preedy)

131) A sad and sorry sight at 81F Oxford on 20th March 1966. Vandals have smashed the windows of the redundant coaling plant and also the windows of the withdrawn pioneer member of the GWR *Modified Hall* Class 4-6-0's No 6959 *Peatling Hall*, dumped, awaiting removal for scrapping. Condemned at Oxford, its home shed, in December 1965, *Peatling Hall* was towed to Cashmores, Newport for scrapping in May 1966. (Mike Wood)

132) As a complete contrast to the above picture, new (if only temporary) life was being implemented into two steam locomotives at Cowlairs Works on 30th August 1966. Undergoing an apparent major overhaul was LMS Class 5 4-6-0 No 45357, from 67A Corkerhill (Glasgow). This proved to be of little future help to 45357 as it was withdrawn four months later. By coincidence BR Class 5 4-6-0 No 73096, see plate 129, was also present. (N. E. Preedy)

133)   LNER B1 Class 4-6-0 No 61330 (62A Thornton Junction) had its work cut out on 1st September 1966, in charge of a single brakevan, as it 'surged' past the camera at Thornton. It was probably on its way to pick up a string of mineral wagons for or from the Fife coalfield. Allocated to Thornton Junction from 64A St. Margarets (Edinburgh) in May 1957, 61330 was an ever present engine at Thornton until condemned in November 1966. (N. E. Preedy)

134)   1966 was the last year for steam domination over the system on the Isle of Wight and also the last year for the route to Newport and Cowes. SR 02 Class 0-4-4T No 20 *Shanklin* (70H Ryde) passes Smallbrook Junction signalbox with a Ventnor to Ryde local in July 1966. The long since severed line, in the right of the picture, to Havenstreet, may well be restored in the not too distant future, if a planned project succeeds. (G. W. Sharpe)

135) A splendid view, as photographed from one of the bedrooms of the Junction Hotel, Tebay, of the lower slope of Shap on 12th May 1966. Sweeping down the incline with a southbound fitted freight is BR *Britannia* Class 4-6-2 No 70041 *Sir John Moore*, from 12A Carlisle (Kingmoor). In the foreground, a rake of enclosed vans occupy the remaining tracks of the long defunct line to Kirkby Stephen. (N. E. Preedy)

136) LNER A2 Class 4-6-2 No 60532 *Blue Peter*, from 62B Dundee Tay Bridge, but sporting a 61B Aberdeen (Ferryhill) shedplate, was in the process of being turned on the turntable at 12A Carlisle (Kingmoor) on 3rd September 1966. *Blue Peter*, in immaculate external condition, was participating in a last A2 Railtour organised by British Railways. It was withdrawn three months later for preservation. (N. E. Preedy)

137) 9K Bolton based BR Class 5 4-6-0 No 73026, in steam in the shed yard at 8F Springs Branch Wigan on 14th July 1966. As was the norm by now, 73026 was devoid of number and shedplates. Once the property of the Western Region and former WR sheds such as Leamington Spa, Shrewsbury and Tyseley, 73026, fitted unusually with a chime whistle, was transferred to Bolton in May 1966, ending its life there, in April 1967. (C. P. Stacey)

138) Amidst heavily wooded and rather attractive scenery, LMS Class 5 4-6-0 No 45395, allocated to 8F Springs Branch Wigan, has steam to spare as it was about to negotiate the pointwork at Dryclough Junction, Halifax, with a Saturdays only, Bradford to Bridlington express, packed with expectant holidaymakers on 9th July 1966. 45395 was drafted to 8A Edge Hill (Liverpool) in December 1967, being withdrawn from there in March 1968. (N. E. Preedy)

139)   Bright sunlight filters into the 'open' roundhouse at 2E Saltley in January 1967. The future for steam at Saltley was not so bright, with the end coming on 6th March, a few short weeks away. One of the few remaining locally based LMS Class 8F 2-8-0's No 48645 simmers in the shadows by the turntable. 48645 was transferred to 6A Chester after the closure of Saltley to steam. Note the Midland Railway STOP notice, issued in April 1922. (Mike Turner)

140) Within a matter of days, the sights and sounds of steam on the Southern were to come to an end. Although devoid of nameplates, a highly polished SR Rebuilt *Merchant Navy* Class 4-6-2 No 35008 *Orient Line*, a local engine, stood proudly on the coaling road at 70A Nine Elms on 7th July 1967. For many years a Bournemouth engine, *Orient Line* had been drafted to 70G Weymouth in October 1966 and to Nine Elms in March 1967. (D. Titheridge)

141) The summer of 1967 saw plenty of steam activity over the West Coast Main Line from Crewe to Carlisle and photographers galore made their way to Shap to observe and capture on camera steam's last fling up this famous gradient. In July 1967, BR *Britannia* Class 4-6-2 No 70031 *Byron*, from Carlisle (Kingmoor), minus nameplates and fitted with a home-made numberplate, was noted at the head of a short parcels train. (Mike Turner)

142) In brilliant sunshine a filthy WD Class 8F 2-8-0 No 90633 (56F Low Moor) threaded its way, tender-first, through a maze of tracks at Laisterdyke (Bradford), with a train of mineral empties on 10th May 1967. The station at Laisterdyke had closed the previous year. 90633, allocated to Low Moor from 56A Wakefield in January 1967, was to live on at Low Moor for less than two months after this picture was taken. (N. E. Preedy)

143) With a wisp of steam drifting lazily from the safety valves, former North Eastern Railway J27 Class 0-6-0 No 65892, from 52G Sunderland, rattles over the ornate large girder bridge at Monkwearmouth, tender-first, with a Class 8 mineral train in July 1967. 65892 was withdrawn from Sunderland depot in August of this same year, being cut up by Willoughby's of Choppington, four months later. (Mike Turner)

144) The last day of steam on the Southern at 70A Nine Elms on 8th July 1967. For SR Rebuilt *West Country* Class 4-6-2 No 34047 *Callington*, late of 70F Bournemouth, the end had already arrived. Its last fire had been drawn the previous month and never again would steam pulse through the powerful cylinders. Built in November 1946 and rebuilt in November 1958, *Callington* was awaiting its last journey to the breakers yard. (F. Hornby)

145) 12A Carlisle (Kingmoor) had some six months or so to go before the sounds of everyday steam servicing and maintenance were to cease forever. There was still plenty of activity at the shed on 17th June 1967, despite the fact that its fleet of engines was diminishing weekly. In steam in the yard on this day was LMS Class 4 'Flying Pig' 2-6-0 No 43121, which had been a Kingmoor engine since June 1965. (D. Titheridge)

146)   Eight members of the LMS *Jubilee* Class 4-6-0's survived into 1967, all on the North Eastern Region, based at sheds in the Bradford, Leeds and Wakefield areas. One of their number, No 45647 *Sturdee*, from 55A Leeds (Holbeck), laid a smoke-screen as it blasted through Bradford with an unidentified express working. In good external condition, *Sturdee's* front end had been 'bulled' up by enthusiasts. (Mike Turner)

147)   8C Speke Junction, in Liverpool, on 18th February 1967. By this date in time the vast majority of surviving steam locomotives at this shed were from the BR Class 9F 2-10-0's. Noted in steam in the yard on this date were three examples of the Class, the centre one being No 92022, a former Crosti version, soon to be transferred to the other side of the river Mersey to 8H Birkenhead. 92022 was condemned in November 1967. (N. E. Preedy)

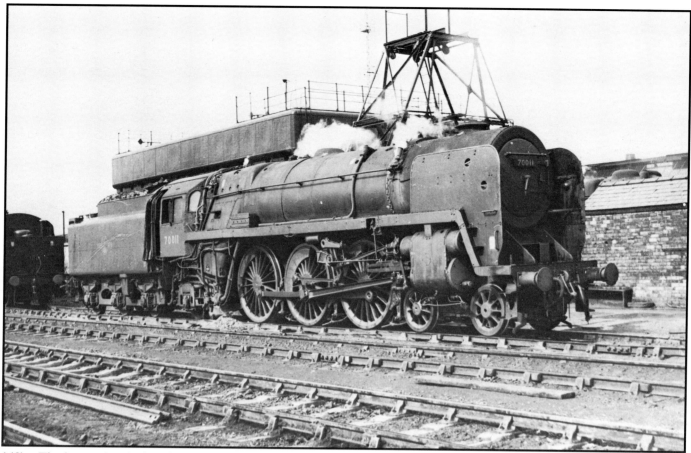

148)   The last major duties allocated to the BR *Britannia* Class 4-6-2's, were on relief express duties, between Crewe and Carlisle. By the summer of 1967 nearly thirty examples of the class were still on active service, all based at 12A Carlisle (Kingmoor). No 70011 *Hotspur*, minus nameplates, takes a rest between duties, in the shed yard at 5B Crewe (South) on 2nd June 1967. *Hotspur* was withdrawn from Kingmoor in December 1967. (N. E. Preedy)

149)   Enjoying the late spring sunshine, the driver and fireman look forward from the cab of their mount, an elderly ex. NER J27 Class 0-6-0 No 65789, from 52G Sunderland, whilst on shunting duties at Morpeth, on the East Coast Main Line, on 26th May 1967. 65789 had two further months to live, being condemned in July 1967. Scrapping came at the hands of Messrs. Hughes Bolckows Ltd., North Blyth in November 1967. (M. Rutter)

150) The sidings adjacent to the shed building at 10D Lostock Hall, Preston, often accommodated condemned steam locomotives, which from time to time were further humbled by the actions of vandals. On 8th July 1967 there was such a line-up of engines, dumped, awaiting their last trip to the scrap merchants, two of them being LMS Fairburn Class 4 2-6-4T No 42224 and BR Class 2 2-6-0 No 78041. (Christopher Fifield)

151) A sad scene at the once mighty 70A Nine Elms on 7th July 1967. Weeds sprout up amidst cold piles of discarded ash and the depot was all but devoid of active engines. Some of the locomotives on view can be identified as LMS Class 2 2-6-2T No 41284, BR Class 4 2-6-4T No 80145, BR Class 4 2-6-0 No 76064, SR Rebuilt *West Country* Class 4-6-2 No 34008 *Padstow* and SR Rebuilt *Merchant Navy* Class 4-6-2 No 35007 *Aberdeen Commonwealth*. (D. Titheridge)

152) A variety of spotters, some of whom were enjoying the relative comfort of a brick wall, crowd one of the platforms at Leeds City in April 1967 as LMS Class 5 4-6-0 No 45219 threw up a vertical pall of black smoke whilst attempting to start an express out of the station. 45219 in suitably begrimed condition has a crudely painted 55A 'shedplate' on the smokebox. (Mike Turner)

153) A soot-stained workhorse from the ageing fleet of ex. North Eastern Railway Q6 Class 0-8-0's No 63426, from 52H Tyne Dock, with a badly scorched and dented smokebox, churns out black smoke as it traversed a labyrinth of tracks at Ryehope Grange Junction, Sunderland with a rake of coke empties on 14th June 1967. 63426 was taken out of service from Sunderland the following month and cut up three months later. (N. E. Preedy)

154) Despite being hemmed in by the third rails, steam still survived at Basingstoke on 13th May 1967. Alive amongst the diesels were two Bulleid Pacifics, the nearest one being SR Rebuilt *Merchant Navy* Class 4-6-2 No 35030 *Elder Dempster Lines*, from 70A Nine Elms. Being a hot looking day, after their shed visit, perhaps some of the elder members of the group would have retired to the nearby *Rising Sun* pub for a pint. (D. Titheridge)

155) Manchester (Victoria) in high summer in 1967. LMS Class 5 4-6-0 No 44891 (9D Newton Heath) acts as a station pilot and was awaiting its next banking duty. Chalked on the tender of 44891 is the statement 'Home Rule for Lancs'. 44891 had been based at Newton Heath for many years and was to remain there until made surplus to requirements when the shed closed on 1st July 1968. (Christopher Fifield)

156) A dishevelled former Crosti-boilered BR Class 9F 2-10-0 No 92025, from 8H Birkenhead, pauses at Northwich station with a lengthy fitted freight in June 1967. Part of the shed yard at Northwich, coded 8E, can be seen in the left of this picture, with a row of LMS Class 8F 2-8-0's in the distance. Northwich was to remain an isolated bastion of steam until early March 1968. (G. W. Sharpe)

157) The depot at 52G Sunderland consisted of a roundhouse and a straight shed. Gathered around the turntable in the former structure on 11th June 1967 were, from left to right, four members of the ex. NER J27 Class 0-6-0's Nos 65804, 65894, 65855 and 65879. All were still active on this date but with the end of steam on the immediate horizon on the North Eastern Region, all four engines were soon to be withdrawn. (N. E. Preedy)

158)   The sole surviving BR *Britannia* Class 4-6-2 No 70013 *Oliver Cromwell* (10A Carnforth) spent more of its time hauling enthusiasts specials in its last few months of active service than it did on other duties. As a result it was always to be seen in immaculate external condition. With a horde of steam enthusiasts hanging out of the carriage windows, *Oliver Cromwell* blasts up the gradient at Copy Pit with a joint Society special on 21st July 1968. (N. E. Preedy)

159) LMS Class 5 4-6-0 No 45104 basks in bright sunshine in the yard of its home shed at 9K Bolton in May 1968. Peeping out from the gloomy shed interior is sister engine No 45110, also based at Bolton. When the shed closed on 1st July 45104 was condemned but 45110 was transferred to 10A Carnforth. A final transfer took 45110 to 10D Lostock Hall from whence it was withdrawn for preservation in August 1968. (Christopher Fifield)

160) The lines around Rose Grove were a mecca for steam enthusiasts during the final months of normal working. A heat haze shimmers off the embankment as LMS Class 8F 2-8-0 No 48278 (10F Rose Grove) neared its home base with a fully laden mineral train on 14th July 1968. Withdrawn upon the closure of the shed on 5th August, 48278 lay in store there for three months before being taken away for scrapping. (N. E. Preedy)

161) The former Cheshire Lines Railway shed at 9F Trafford Park had been closed for almost a month when this photograph was taken on 3rd June 1968. Amidst a deathly silence, two forlorn LMS Class 8F 2-8-0's, the nearest one being No 48107, lie cold and still, never to turn their wheels again in revenue earning service. Withdrawn from Heaton Mersey in April 1968, 48107 was cut up at Buttigiegs, Newport three months later (C. P. Stacey)

162) Two LMS Class 5 4-6-0's Nos 45025 and 45390, both from 10A Carnforth, combine to double-head a railtour, near Whalley, between Blackburn and Clitheroe in the Spring of 1968. The station at Whalley had closed to passengers in 1962. Both 45025 and 45390 survived until the end of steam in August 1968. 45025 is now actively preserved on the Strathspey Railway at Aviemore. (Christopher Fifield)

163) Another photograph taken in the Spring of 1968. LMS Class 5 4-6-0 No 44781 (10A Carnforth) arrives at its home base with a short freight of coal wagons. 44781 had lost its front number and shedplate but these had been replaced by stencilled lettering. This engine, along with 44871, was later to double-head the final BR steam special between Carlisle and Manchester on 11th August 1968. (Christopher Fifield)

164) Despite looking in reasonable external order at first glance, it was the end of the road for LMS Class 8F 2-8-0 No 48492, as can be seen by the missing coupling rods. 48492, withdrawn from 10D Lostock Hall in February 1968, was dumped on the 'condemned' road at the shed on 20th April 1968. A final journey the following month took 48492 for cutting up at Drapers, Hull. (C. Richards)

165)   Like BR *Britannia* Class 4-6-2 No 70013 *Oliver Cromwell*, BR Class 5 4-6-0 No 73069 was the last working survivor of
        its class and it too was based at 10A Carnforth, where it was photographed in the shed yard in late July 1968. It also
        survived until the end of working steam but unlike *Oliver Cromwell* it was not destined for preservation. The end for 73069
        came at Cashmores, Newport in March 1969. (G. W. Sharpe)

166)   Bolton in May 1968 and steam could still be seen from time to time, mostly on freight duties. A locally based LMS Class
        8F 2-8-0 No 48319 drifts towards the camera with a long rake of coal trucks from the Manchester direction. Within a
        matter of days, the shed died, as did 48319 along with many sister engines. Like many a victim before, 48319 was destroyed
        at the hands of Drapers, Hull. (Christopher Fifield)

167) An attempt had been made to spruce up the external lines of LMS Class 8F 2-8-0 No 48033, from 9H Patricroft, which was the subject of much admiration at Manchester (Victoria) on 23rd June 1968. 48033 was being employed on the Locomotive Club of Great Britain inspired, *Two Cities Limited*, complete with a smart headboard and badges, presumably the Coats of Arms of Liverpool and Manchester. (N. E. Preedy)

168) 8C Speke Junction on 6th April 1968, one month before closure to steam. In the left of the picture are a brace of BR Class 9F 2-10-0's, the nearest being No 92218, fitted with a double chimney. To the right of 92218, a Speke Junction engine, is LMS Class 8F 2-8-0 No 48191, a visitor from 9F Heaton Mersey. (Mike Wood)

169) LMS Class 5 4-6-0 No 45386, from 10D Lostock Hall, waits for the road at Colne, Lancashire, with a fitted freight on 14th June 1968. Colne, used to be situated halfway between Burnley and Skipton, with regards to the rail scene, until the section to Skipton was closed in 1970. 45386 was another engine which lasted to the end of steam, ending up in the clutches of Drapers, Hull, in April 1969. (N. E. Preedy)

170) BR Class 4 4-6-0 No 75048, a visitor from 10A Carnforth, in steam in company with an unidentified LMS Class 8F 2-8-0, in the shed yard at 10F Rose Grove on 20th April 1968. 75048, once a longstanding resident of 27A Bank Hall, had been transferred to 6C Croes Newydd (Wrexham) in May 1966. It moved on to Carnforth in June 1967 when Croes Newydd closed to steam. (N. E. Preedy)

171)   A final look at 9K Bolton shed on 1st June 1968. LMS Class 8F 2-8-0 No 48168 was photographed in steam by the coaling plant prior to taking up a freight working. When the shed closed, many of the drivers, firemen and other shed staff would be thrown on the scrap heap, just like the locomotives they once proudly manned. 48168 went to Drapers, Hull for cutting up in September 1968. (N. E. Preedy)

172)   LMS Class 5 4-6-0 No 45350, from 10F Rose Grove, sports a resurrected 26A Newton Heath shedcode, for old times sake, although it was never based there in the sixties, as it sped towards the camera at Darwen, between Blackburn and Bolton, on 15th June 1968 with a Saturdays only Colne to Manchester parcels train. Rendered surplus to requirements in August 1968, 45350 was cut up at Wards, Beighton, Sheffield in December 1968. (N. E. Preedy)

CHAPTER TEN – SCRAPYARDS

173) With the nameplates long since removed, LNER B1 Class 4-6-0 No 61248 *Geoffrey Gibbs*, late of 40E Colwick, lies in a sorry state at Hughes Bolckows Ltd., North Blyth on 26th February 1966 prior to cutting up two months later. *Geoffrey Gibbs*, once based at 40A Lincoln and 40B Immingham, had been transferred to Colwick from Immingham in January 1965 being withdrawn from there in November of the same year. (M. Rutter)

174) In the 1950's locomotives withdrawn from service were usually cut up for scrap at the main works of their parent company. The remains of former Lancashire & Yorkshire Class 2F 0-6-0ST No 51513 had almost disappeared into the waiting wagons when this photograph was taken at Horwich Works on Sunday, 27th May 1956. Note the Sunday working – after some overtime no doubt. (J. D. Gomersall)

175) Awaiting the 'chop' at Barry Docks on 16th April 1969 were SR Rebuilt *West Country* Class 4-6-2 No 34046 *Braunton*, SR Unrebuilt *Battle of Britain* Class 4-6-2 No 34070 *Manston*, SR U Class 2-6-0 No 31806 and three Diesel Hydraulic locomotives Nos D6122, D600 *Active* and D601 *Ark Royal*. For a change it is the steam engines which had the last laugh, with all three being saved for posterity. (Ken Ellis)

176) A line of condemned locomotives await the inevitable at Birds, Long Marston, near Stratford-upon-Avon on 20th March 1966. Most of the engines are of former Great Western origin – a 5600 Class 0-6-2T and a 5100 Class 2-6-2T – unidentified. Nearest the camera is 5700 Class 0-6-0PT No 3788 which had been withdrawn from 2B Oxley in November 1965 following an accident near Stourbridge. (Mike Wood)

CHAPTER ELEVEN – PRESERVED LOCOMOTIVES

177)   On Sunday 7th August 1988, 'Pathfinder Tours' – *Yorkshire Venturer*, took Class 50 No 50037 *Illustrious* from Swindon to York. The second leg of the journey was taken over by BR Class 9F 2-10-0 No 92220 *Evening Star* from York to Scarborough and on to Hull. We see *Evening Star* in immaculate condition, awaiting for departure from Scarborough. On arrival at Hull, *Illustrious* took over for the return trip to Swindon. (C. Richards)